Tim Clare is the author of the p
We Can't All Be Astronauts and
solo stage shows, which he has ..
He is one of the UK's most popular stand-up poets
and a familiar face at both literary and music festivals.

Pub Stuntman

Tim Clare

Nasty Little Press

Published by Nasty Little Press in July 2012.

Nasty Little Press
35 St Johns Road, Bungay, Suffolk, NR35 1DH
nastylittlepress.org
@nastylit

ISBN: 978-0-9573000-0-2

Set in Book Antiqua. Printed and bound by MPG Biddles

A CIP record of this book is available
from the British Library.

To Lisa

Contents

PUB STUNTMAN

Welcome To The Poetry Arena

Roll up, roll up! We're about to get started!
Dip in your toe! Take a seat in our shrine.
Don't be afraid, it's all right, no one's farted,
you'll just have to hear the odd poem or... nine.
Come in, dear friends! Quit your timid conjectures!
Tarry no longer! Please, pull up a pew!
Commit to a stream of interminable lectures
from people who think they're much smarter than you!
Welcome, hello – brush the grass from your jeans,
I've just been explaining what 'patronise' means.
We say what you're thinking – we do it in rhyme!
Sit down, shut up, cos it's poetry time.

Look at those reprobates out in the sunshine
talking out loud while they listen to bands!
Real art's not meant to be *fun*, you damn philistines!
Look at this gentleman, he understands.
This is a haven of learning and prudence,
(it's like being trapped in a lift full of students)
some of us might even read off the page!
Oh – thank you God! It's the Poetry Stage!

We might not be rich, we might not be famous,
we might not be even particularly good,
but we're so much *better* than mere entertainers
don't watch for enjoyment – just watch cos you should!

Linger no longer, step out of the weather,
come and appreciate poems forever!
Perhaps, if you're lucky, you'll hear a sestina.
Arty or what? It's the Poesy Arena!

Give us your love! We were none of us breastfed!
(Except for a few who were breastfed too long)
I use big words! Jesus! Aren't you impressed yet?
If poems make sense then you're doing it wrong.
Here's a ghazal – you won't understand it.
I thought I'd compile a few musings on trees.
This is a piece I call: ULTIMATE SOUL PAIN.
Who coughed at the back then? Gentlemen, please!
Step inside friends, stop and smell the azaleas,
here comes an endless procession of failures
their spleens to explosively, rhythmically vent!
Come one, come... one, to the Poetry Tent.

I'd Like To Take This Opportunity
To Introduce Myself

This is my scrimshaw chess set
and this is my hat -
see how the fine brim doubles
as a mischief balustrade.

I stiffen my felt death warrant
with mercury. This is my pet
barrister, Stephen Quinn.
Say hello, Stephen.

This is the standard waiver
I give to all new acquaintances.
This is a painting of some breakfast.
Think nothing of it.

This is my left glove.
As you can see
I am wearing it on my right hand.
I am something of a practical joker.

This is Stephen's first attempt at batik.
I realise it looks like a bloodied handkerchief.
Don't panic!
This is my bloodied handkerchief.

This is my fob watch.
This is my monogrammed cigarette case.
(the 'N' stands for 'nostril')
This is my dog fossil.

This is my memoir.
This is my maxim:
Time heals all wounds,
so why bother with hospitals?

Armadillo

The armadillo arrives in the parcel chute
with a clank; a medicine ball, curled up,
a clump of dense-packed raffia, a Moses
basket with a dead shrew in it.
There is no return address.

Andrew brought in a box of Ferrero Rocher
(today is his 31st birthday)
and we sit, glancing
from our half eaten chocolates
to the armadillo cadaver,
chewing. No one wants to touch it.

Walking home that night, we kick unshelled conkers
with nihilistic gusto,
the full moon a headache pulsing
in a sky of glass dust.

We all hope that, by tomorrow, the corpse will be gone,
its questions shuffled back into the deck,
our uneasiness bricked over, like a fireplace.

In Which You Are Decapitated On A Rollercoaster In Budapest

You are decapitated on a rollercoaster in Budapest.
A year later I write about it.
The poem starts with me and you eating chimney cake
at a Hungarian fair.

The boy who sells it to us wears a red scarf like a bandage,
his cakes lined up in a wicker basket.
One day he'll go to university, learn computer science
and end up designing a database that's used in hospitals.

I tell the reader this as a way of building dramatic tension
because everyone's waiting for the moment
when a broken stanchion clubs your head
clean from your shoulders.
We all know it's coming
because the poem is called:
'In Which My Significant Other Gets Decapitated
On A Rollercoaster'.

A headless lover
makes everything resonant.
I tease the crowd with metaphor:
a coconut shy, a scoop of peach ice cream
falling soft and spherical
onto poignant frost-tinged ground.

The poem tells of biting into chimney cake,
pastry cracking like pond ice,
the sting of cinnamon like a tot of whiskey.
I write about the weeks that come after,
about giving your books to the charity shop
then regretting it,
the loneliness of finding a glove in the garden,
grief's raw boredom.

Near the end of the poem I write about you
getting your head knocked off.
My account is clinical,
passionate, triumphant.
Critics hail its mordant brilliance.
It becomes an instant addition to every syllabus,
your head detaching from your body
over and over in lecture halls up and down the country,
the soft whump like a thumped punchball
in ten thousand students' heads,
my stanza on the red cockscomb splatter pattern
committed to memory and regurgitated
in exams, recalled with a shudder
fifteen years later, while watching a winter sunset
or wiping raspberry puree
from a toddler's cheeks.

In the closing third of the poem,
I imagine writing about your death –
how it wins national poetry competitions

and becomes the title piece of my first collection,
Big Wheel.
I perform it all round the country
at independent bookshops and packed literary events,
accruing the signifiers of highbrow caché like Pokémon.

After each amber-lit reading,
strangers bestow mercy fucks
with the urgency of paramedics,
excited perhaps
by my description of arterial gushing,
nauseous at their own mortality.
Let's have vigorous sex
before we too are beheaded,
their sweaty, out of focus faces
seem to say.

In the final stanzas of the poem
and the poem within the poem,
and in this poem,
I wake up on the rollercoaster,
your head intact,
only this time
a snapped strut does not fall like a clapperboard across the track.
We ride out the troughs and bell curves together,
our carriage slows and stops like a nosebleed
and a man in a carpet coat smoking a cigarette
steps forward and lifts the bar from our chests.

I do not stagger from my seat,
anaesthetised with wonder,
touching the ground, touching my skin.
You look unsurprised to be alive –
complacent, even –
and I can't help but notice
the way your head sits
between your shoulders
like a cannonball,
like a winter moon,
a Christmas pudding.

The Unemployed Hangman

He sits on a park bench, glum as a duck,
meaty hand gripping an empty noose.

An old lady in a green duffel coat approaches him.
'What's wrong?' she coos. 'Have you

lost your dog?' His stubbled head lifts
like a boulder rolling back.

'Something like that.'
He heaves a sigh.

'Well, I'll be sure to keep an eye out, dear.
My dog ran off just last year.

He can be ever so naughty.'
The man's face brightens.

'How naughty?' he says,
fingering his rope.

Be Kind To Yourself

Be kind to yourself.
Each day, give yourself a compliment.
Make it specific,
one you've always wanted to receive:
'Your seafood risotto is ace.'
'That time after salsa class
when you bought everyone ice cream
was magical.'
'Thanks for doing the washing up
for four weeks
after Dad's funeral.'

Be kind to yourself.
Learn the art of disappointing people;
the bar will manage Friday night without you;
Ross can wait another day to play ping-pong;
your daughter will have other clarinet recitals
or, more likely,
she will take the hint and give up.

Be kind to yourself.
Make yourself a full Christmas dinner with all the
trimmings
in the middle of July,
gravy, cranberry sauce
and big glasses of port.

Afterwards, doze off on the sofa in front of Shrek 3
and when your boss calls
to ask why you aren't at work today
ask him who the fuck he thinks he is,
calling you on today of all days?
Apologise. This is the season of goodwill.
Invite him round for mince pies and sherry,
about sixish?
Tell him yes, you are feeling okay,
you're just learning how to be happy in a world
made mostly of gas and dying meat.
Your boss will offer you the rest of the week off.
Take it
like the last Quality Street.

Be kind to yourself.
Snatch a charity tin
from an old lady
collecting money for the Lifeboat Appeal
and use the proceeds to fill your fridge
with 50 tubes of Smarties.
I know they're made by Nestle
but come on,
it's not like you're stealing
charity tins from old ladies
oh wait ...

Be kind to yourself.
Sleep with people

other than your wife –
you deserve it.
After all, you spent a whole afternoon
creosoting the new shed
while she sat on a lawn chair
reading *My Booky Wook 2*.
When she discovers your infidelity
she will probably say:
'Fair play, mate,'
laugh, and slap you on the back.
Yes, it's what I'd do.

Be kind to yourself.
Stop leaving the house.
Outdoors there is weather and cat mess.
Why put yourself through that
when there's leftover turkey right here
under the coffee table?
Let answerphone messages stack up
like song requests on a pub jukebox.
Drink the last 100ml of sherry,
then play 'Jingle Bell Rock' at full blast
on the downstairs stereo,
dancing like a toddler
while the neighbours hammer their approval
against the partition wall.

Be kind to yourself.
Let friendships drop like pine needles.

Save on laundry by wearing nothing
but a powder blue dressing gown.
Allow yourself to come unmoored
from the sun's glum, luckless circuits.
Leave the lights off, and walk
through your house at 2am.
You will feel like a ghost
haunting scenes from his old life,
unwashed plates heaped in the sink like manuscripts,
a dim, mauve diamond of moonlight
picking out fridge magnets
and an obsolete to-do list.
Drink the last 5ml of port.
Call your ex-wife
and listen to her breathing
before she hangs up.
She will be strangely unreal,
like an urban fox caught in a porch light.

Be kind to yourself.
Lie flat on the cool, sticky kitchen floor,
your dressing gown soft as terry towelling.
Drink the brandy you were saving for best.
You are excellent at noticing life's little absurdities.
Well done for creosoting the shed.
Your beard smells like Christmas.
You are a brilliant whistler.

Down With The Kids

The past is another country,
a crap one, like Belgium,
rife with brown-trousered tedium
where no one sees disasters coming,
where the phones are big as bricks,
where men sleepwalk down aisles with their future ex-wives,
where the only telly is repeats.

But don't slag it off
cos I was born on those streets!
Where my gawky demeanour and penchant for munching
made my peers jeer 'Oi speccy! Oi sumo! Oi bumchin!
I heard that the bruise on your tricep needs punching
now don't you go dream of amounting to something!
I told you last Tuesday – or hasn't it sunk in?'
These lads who led lives of fags, football and spunking
who sat their exams and got straight As (in flunking).

While girls deft as surgeons sat squeezing their blackheads
all strung out on burgeoning hormones like crackheads.
They used boys like me for their sarcasm practice.
I vied for one girl who seemed gentle and kindly,
an angel, she'd surely have never maligned me,
she'd never go '*Dickhead!*' or '*Wanker!*' behind me...
Oh, the rolled eyes and wrinkle-nosed dry gagging gesture
she did to her friends when I tried to impress her,

as if she'd been licked by some rough-tongued molester
like Caliban came from his cave to caress her
or hordes of black locusts had tried to undress her -
'Get back to your books and Nintendo, professor!'

And so I slammed shut
like a vault
or a clam
like a Transformer morphing back into a van.

Fast forward
to now
and my ego's intact,
I've seen a girl naked
(seen several, in fact).
I keep my achievements impressively stacked
and when I'm a twat, well, it's part of my act.

And one day, I wake up in a scene from my dreams:
I'm up on a stage and the crowd's mostly teens
and so mustering all my newfound self-esteem
I think: Right – *time to show these kids just what 'cool' means.*

I thought they'd like me,
I thought they'd admire me,
I thought they'd be inspired.
Aspire to be like me like I was some guy off the telly.

I thought they might at least, you know,
smile politely.

Oh, in my head, how they'd applaud!
They laughed and howled and cheered!
But in real life I got ignored
cos they thought I was weird.
The kids all sat there looking bored,
they made me feel a crooked fraud
till something deep inside me roared:
I will not take this anymore-d.

Okay, I'm not 'down with the kids'
so I say:
Down with the kids!
Drown 'em like a sack of philistine kittens!
The kid gloves are off,
it's on
with the man-mittens.

I don't wanna be cool,
I wanna be a curmudgeon.
I'll speak at your school
with its fresh dreams to bludgeon:

'The Oxford English Dictionary defines "teenager" as
Buhhhhh! Uhhhh!
Aged 13 to 17.

You young minds who sit before me today
are rubbish!
You download your rubbish opinions like ringtones,
stuff rubbish maize snacks into bum-fluff edged gobs.
A putrefied mackerel smell wafts from your pissy bits,
you lurch between fury, indifference and sobs.
Your clichéd McHeartbreak, your shrill swine-faced hissy fits,
your feelings are rubbish,
glum zit-witted yobs.
And even if one of you does become an astronaut
the infinite void will press its thumb against your tiny visor
and not let go till you're A JOYLESS ATHEIST!

You still think death is other people.

Children
(huge, freakish, ungainly children)
you need to think about death more.
I remember that I'm going to die
at least five times before breakfast
(which I take at 2pm
in my underpants
playing *Super Mario Sunshine* on the Gamecube
while you're stuck in a classroom that stinks of pencils)
And what do I have for my breakfast?
Whatever I like!
Pork pies in gravy
and Poppets
and booze!

I can eat what I want!
I can drink when I choose!
Oh, I think I'll consume this huge vat of red wine
so I'm rat-arsed in time for the 3 O'Clock News.'

So fuck the kids
(well, don't *fuck* the kids)
but down with the kids!
Get off my lawn!
You've never heard of Teletext?
You don't even know you're born!
With your wi-mo i-hood my-isode nanos
and your ability to hear through the ears in your knees!
No wait
I'm thinking of crickets. Yes...

Their chirruping wing strokes as teens sit in judgement
as gag after quip after joke I make tanks.
Grip my mic, but I know where they'd like me to stick it,
their faces as hard as a concrete abutment,
their afternoons measured in texting and wanks.
So go on then, don't love me! I don't need your approval!
I'd sooner fork out for a bollock removal
and if you should come crawling back on your knees
bearing blog hits and Friend Requests begging me: 'Please!
Without you the whole world is greyer and colder!
Look! Jenny has Tippexed your name on her folder!'
I'll shake my head slow in the warm changing breeze,
'No,' I'll say, smiling. 'Not till you're older.'

Pub Stuntman

The bedside table's finest teak,
its curlicues pretentious,
my glass is full of scotch and ice,
her glass contains her dentures.
Her lips are dry, her legs are splayed,
she switches off her hearing aid
then, famished as a zombie queen,
regards me with her one real eye.
She winks, she grins,
her grey gums bleed
we do the deed,
we do the deed.
The yellowed nails, the wheezing breaths,
the stink of stale saliva,
but all that I can think of is:
Heh.
Dave owes me a fiver.

Cos some men live for politics
and some men live for romance,
but me, I live for running down
the high street wearing no pants.
I'm quite the character, you see,
and one day I'll be famous,
now film me while I light the
Roman candle in my anus.

Chaps and lasses! Raise a glass
to idiocy's frontman!
I have no shame, I feel no pain,
pray silence, for Pub Stuntman.

There's nothing that I wouldn't down,
a pint glass my inverted crown!
Attention is my favourite noun!
Or... 'bumtackle'
what a blunt man!
Tuesday means tequila bender!
Come on, liver! No surrender!
Look, a girl – let's go offend her!
Crass remark based on your gender
Watch me lick a sticking plaster!
I do things the smart say *naaah* to:
fart half the Moonlight Sonata?
Ha ha – that's the sound I'm after!

This bar is my Vegas,
every stunt I pull's a flutter,
and if laughter's the best medicine:
I'm drinking Calpol in the gutter!

Here's my gonads – pass the lighter!
Twist these fluffy handcuffs tighter!
Pass that vase of Jaegermeister,
ring my grandma – let's invite her!
Punters gather round to see me –

Look! I'm like those blokes on TV.
50p to drink some wee wee?
That'll sound good on my CV.
Take a drawing pin and spike me!
Fill your socks with sand and strike me!
Stub a fag out on my knob,
just please God, like me. *Please.*

I'll do a bet, I'll do a dare,
down Guinness mixed with pubic hair,
as long as you all stop and stare,
just stop and stare,
just stop and stare,
it's how I know you really care.

I'd rather be a drunken dunce
than struggle with profound shit.
I almost had a feeling once
but grabbed a shot and drowned it.
And yes, the mess impressed them
when I burnt off all my anus hair
but every time I lit a fart
I meant to send a rescue flare.
And when I shagged the quiz machine,
and couldn't pull my cock free,
I think what I was trying to say was:
'Please – somebody *stop* me.'

A human hid inside this prat,
I smothered him with clowning.
I was much too far out all my life,
and not waving,

                    but downing.

In The Unlikely Event Many Of My Victims'
Bodies Remain Unaccounted For

Here are the solutions to last Wednesday's killing spree:
most you found the body of Ms Ethel K Wildgust
in the water closet of a houseboat in Ely.
'Asphyxiated with a rubber hose' several of you guessed,
a few others went for 'drowned';
well, I can put you out of your misery, the answer was in fact
'smothered with her late husband's overcoat'.
Well done to those of you who got that one.

Our 'Exquisite Corpse' was a real stumper this week,
so congratulations to A H Tudor of Walton-on-the-Naze
who correctly identified the chimera
dumped near a lay-by on the A534
as a composite stitched together from parts of
Mr J Kilby of Tiverton,
Miss T R Kilby of Hastings (no relation)
and Mr L Hernandez of Welwyn Garden City.
A H Tudor – not sure if that's a man or a woman –
receives a thirty pound Waterstones book token.

Speaking of which,
they say the best place to hide a book
is in a library,
but it seems the best place to hide a corpse
is in a library;

none of you spotted
Mr N Jackson of Tewksbury
propped in a chair by the magazine racks,
stuck on page 132 of *Sons And Lovers* for six days now,
a heavy tweed hunting coat disguising
his fatal sabre-wound.

Several of you wrote in, delighted
at having found the smashed cadaver
of Robert Tomlinson
at the foot of the NCP multi-storey carpark
in Newport.
Sorry to disappoint you,
but it was self-inflicted
after an argument with his fiancée,
so no points there.

Some of you may have already guessed
the hidden theme linking this week's corpses –
it is, of course,
early twentieth-century celebrities
most commonly known by their first two initials:
the corpse in the water closet in meadowy Ely
represents the wonderful entertainer W. C. Fields,
the first letters of the three lay-by victims' hometowns
spell out T H W, or T. H. White,
author of celebrated Arthurian quartet, *The Once And Future King*,
and our library corpse was reading *Sons And Lovers*,
by the late, great, D. H. Lawrence.

In The Unlikely Event You Spot My Face Amidst The Seething Zombie Horde

I expect
when my blue head appeared
in the dead lens of your rifle scope,
it reminded you of the time at Glastonbury
when the camera found us
and we appeared on the big screens,
you on my shoulders in a sea of meat and flags.

If you're reading this,
I hope you haven't shot me.
Yet.

If you're reading this,
you must have found the note
clothes-pegged to my pullover,
flapping sadly like a ghost snagged on a TV aerial.
I wrote it while the bite went nasty.

Look, I know I turned to you
while we were watching *Dawn Of The Dead* and said:
'Sweetheart, if you ever turn zombie
I will straight up shoot you in the face,'
and once during *Wall-E*,
and at your nephew's christening,

and during sex,
but I want you to know I was kidding.
That's why I never smiled.

What I meant was:
'Darling, the day you turn zombie
I will shepherd you home,
shackle you in the cellar
and feed you tinned horsemeat through a hatch,
because I know you'd do the same for me.'

Sweetpea,
look into my eye
(it's hanging just below my chin,
swinging from the optic nerve
like a thick grey teardrop)
I'm the same shambling insomniac
who chased you down stairwells,
who reached for you, endlessly.

I always loved you for your brains.
That hasn't changed.

All I'm asking is,
if you've not already blasted my piñata skull
to pink streamers then please,
take me back.

I'll live in the barricaded basement,
foul and replete,
while you sit on the roof
with your gun and your binoculars,
swinging your legs, celebrity spotting.

The Pranksters

'I've got a bucket of mayonnaise!'
said Barnaby,
returning from the Cash & Carry
with a bucket of mayonnaise.
He slammed it down on the table
sending Rummikub tiles everywhere.
'A bucket of mayonnaise,' Neil laughed,
shaking his onion-shaped head.
'Only a nutter like you
would come back from the Cash & Carry
with a bucket of mayonnaise!'
Barnaby sat on the couch with a can of Lilt.
'I reckon we could get up to some pretty serious mischief
with this.' And they both sat there
grinning at the bucket of mayonnaise.

Hours later,
Neil coughed blood in a lightless alley
while distant sirens wailed.
 'I wish I'd never set eyes on that
bucket of mayonnaise!' he spluttered,
clutching a swatch of wet cardboard
to his sucking chest wound.
'Shh,' said Barnaby,
reloading.

In The Unlikely Event I Stumble Upon
A Shadowy Cabal Of Shapeshifting Lizards

The Home Secretary's throat puffed out like a jug.
He kept one pupil fixed on my revolver,
while the other tracked a mosquito
executing ponderous loops
in the thick, wet air of the hothouse.

His shirt and tie had rumpled in the heat.
I aimed my gun at his abdomen
and asked him what he intended to do
about the government's antiquated drugs policy.
'It's a social and moral issue,
not a criminal justice one,' I said,
reading a statement off my i-Phone.
Then I got a text from Kenny
which spun me out a bit.
'Wait a minute,' I said.
In the raffia palms above our heads,
a macaw said 'chalk.'

When I looked again at the Home Secretary
he was tipping his head back
to gulp down a clutch of crane's eggs.
As they crunched in his gullet
he turned to me with a yolky grimace,
tongue flickering across thin lips.

'I never wanted this,' he said,
brushing shell flecks from his dewlap creases.
'If I had my wish I'd live under the volcano
with the others. They have flat rocks, hot as skillets.'

Outside the hothouse it was almost Christmas.
Every Westminster paving slab
was frictionless as a polished tooth.
'In winter, I harden like a scab.'
From his jacket, he took a small gold box
set on four curved feet.
'Here,' his talon threw the ornate catch,
'you can have the secret drug we keep for ourselves.'

He flipped the lid.
'It lets us maintain our human form.
If a human takes it,' (both times
he spat the word) 'they go back
to the time they were most happy
and get to pilot the memory around
like a helicopter,

landing it in new contexts
like a rainforest, or a Japanese bathhouse,
or the *Cheers* bar, for instance.'
I shot him,
his cranial ridge cracking like a seashell,
and caught the box as it slipped from his claws.
His body thumped to the floor

like an overcoat falling from a bronze hook.
Something black came out his mouth.
I tilted the box towards me
and downed the lot.

A slow dissolve
then we were together again
in the bombed out ruins of a cathedral.
'Who are you?' he said,
and I drew my pistol.
The Home Secretary's throat puffed out like a jug.

Q & A With Maurice Verdier

Q: What can you tell us about the contemporary poetry scene in France?

A: Well, I don't presume to speak for French poets as a whole, but sometimes I sit at the piano, blow the dust off some sheet music, and a hundred sleeping ants scatter like bombed refugees. I once found a stale sponge cake in my piano stool. It was dry as a cuttlefish.

Q: Who are your favourite living French poets?

A: I've always felt drawn to the clamp jars of Sebastian Guillaume – he has a way of cramming a dozen or more chaffinches into a vessel no more than six inches high and four inches in diameter. Then he seals the lid and they're trapped there, twitching, filling the space almost like a liquid. If one catches your eye, the intensity... it's a perfect exchange.

Q: What do you see as the greatest challenges facing contemporary French poets?

A: Well first let me say that I do not view challenges as negative – art is all about confronting, overcoming. So I think that any challenges strengthen us. With that in mind, I would say that the greatest challenge is the large numbers of poets gradually turning to oak. Of course it depends where it starts – Brouillard was able to continue to write for many months while his toes, feet, ankles and lower legs slowly solidified into stiff wooden prosthetics. But once it hardens your lungs or heart... *C'est le fin*, as we say.

In The Unlikely Event I Go Down With The Ship

Since the water is up to my throat now,
here is my wishlist.
        I want a cremation.
        I want it nice and hot –
        the vicar eyebrowless and wincing.
        Scatter my ashes in the faces of children.

The water feels like a liquid poncho;
it is not so cold, due to the fire in the engine room.
It smells coppery.
Its surface is covered with effects:
a purser's ledger,
a fluffy pen topper from Dobwalls' theme park,
the ship's cat; drowned continents
bumping and orbiting like drunk debutants
navigating the plate tectonics
of the ballroom.
        I want a buoy for a headstone,
        clapping its leprous bell in the green mist.
        I want a dozen spike mines,
        bonny as dog toys.

The water is on my bottom lip.
If I say 'Hello' it comes in twice.
If I say 'Bye' it comes in once.

The Scholar

Twas in a dream
The Scholar strode,
The Scholar strode with me,
We walked o'er shale
Through wind and hail
Beside the tumbling sea.
Twas in a dream
Through squall and gale
Beside the tumbling sea.

Beneath our feet, a brittle hoard,
A trove of Neptune's bric-a-brac
By cliffs where Satan walks abroad
A-riding sinners pick-a-back.

And in that dream, we sat a spell
Beyond the bitter waves
'Come, learned sir,' said I, 'and tell
Me how a sage behaves.'
Said I, 'O Scholar, kindly dwell
On how a sage behaves.'

The Scholar's withered fingers curled
His weathered countenance grew grim
As if our sick and sorry world
Had piled its every ounce on him.

He gripped his stick and fished a
Prophylactic from a foggy pool
Then with a frown, he set it down,
Atop a flyblown doggy stool.

A sheath spread in the middle
Of a moist and greenish turd
Said I: 'Is this a riddle?'
But he did not speak a word
A condom in some dog mess
Yet he did not speak a word.

I sat upon the rocks of blue
That lined the frigid shore
And gazed upon the Scholar's poo
For half an hour or more.

What secret did this poo contain?
What meaning lay within?
Until, at last, I cried aghast:
'Enough, sir! I give in!
What secret does this turd hold fast?
Enough, sir! I give in!'

A blankness cloaked the visage
Of this sage of ancient lore
A tiny lump of spinach
Clinging damply to his jaw.
'Come, man of tomes,' said I again,

'How should a sage conduct himself?'
He grasped his cane, then – in clear pain –
He stooped, and gravely fucked himself.

And as I watched the man engage
In urgent auto-sodomy
I mused that much about this sage
Seemed, frankly, rather odd to me.

His feet that splayed contrariwise
His fixed and crooked grin
The slight opaque cast to his eyes
The dribble on his chin
The funny smell, the open flies,
And dribble on his chin.

Said I: 'Uh... this might sound like...
Like a stupid qu...
You are the wise Scholar of...
Ancient lore, aren't you?'

He shook his fat, ungainly head
Bisected by a scar
Then opening his mouth to speak,
The Scholar uttered: 'Gaaaaaaaaaaaaaaaaaaaaaaaaah.'

I left him then
Upon the shore
The waves did crash and hiss

And as I strode
My heart became
A howling, black abyss
I woke at once, at home, alone,
my bed bemired in piss.

Total Destruction To Those Who Laughed At Me And Failed To Heed My Warnings

My sky ark rumbles
through the parting cloudbank
dropping parachute bombs
through a trapdoor in the timber hull

and playing ragtime
through several banks of loudspeakers,
overlaid by invocations
to various minor interventionist deities

and shoutouts:
'*You*, Deborah Nesmith! Who continued to park
in my spot after a polite note
tucked under your windscreen wiper!
You, Horace Golightly! Sprinkling Trill
in my hair during the test match
and believing I would not notice!
You, Lincoln Coops! Who built several effigies
of me in Lego then kicked them in,
laughing all the while, well
who's laughing now you bastard,'

roofs exploding, etc, etc.

In Defence Of Long Poems

If you must know, I find low self-esteem
charming. Haikus have a swagger
that makes me want to dry retch,

like some kimono-clad arts professor
who swans into the party's second room,
announces some recondite maxim then

about-faces, inscrutable smirk
smeared all over his cheeks like jam.
Fuck him

and his lack of stamina
masquerading as high truth. Let us
each in turn follow him out that door

then buttonhole him in a corner
of the kitchen, lecturing him at the length
about the shape of conches

and appalling glue
till he cannot stand
for shrinking.

Ode To The Debonair Rogue Who Cloned My Debit Card

See the dandified Adonis
decked in golden cape and tie
on his way to pen some honest
poetry – o, what a guy!
Hear this cultured upper-cruster
drunk with trinkets, whores, and wine
sharing tales of spunk and bluster
he's one card you can't decline.
Taste his tainted perspiration,
smell his blend of fine colognes:
Eau de Gnawing Desperation,
fag smoke, cordite, pheromones.
Heart of gobshite, grin of God,
Gentleman Poet with a massive wad.

He's all I've ever longed to be
and yet – a bitter irony –
his life is broken binary
where one is him
and zero's me:
'Ah Hortense and Hermione,
I must insist you dine with me.
The Chateau Sixty-Nine, *oui, oui*.
He'll fetch it from the winery.
Two ladies in such finery

I rarely get the time, you see,
It makes one pine so for Paris.
Where is that Gallic swine? Henri!
The staff all take a shine to me,
they'd probably let me dine for free,
they even made a sign for me
with little lines of poetry.
I like to read them as I dine,
don't tell customers they're mine,
don't want attention from the rabble.'
You write verse?
'Well, yes… I dabble.'

O towering colossus!
O Timothy Clare!
Amassing huge losses
at Craps with such flair
then laughing it off
as he tosses his hair
like some high-living, solid-chinned
Charles Baudelaire!
O Timmy J Clare! O Timmy J Clare!
Gifted, uplifted, by talent so rare!
What a singular character I proved to be
when I stole all my money by acting as me.
One thousand, two thousand, O! Sweet creeping fuck!
The grace of a swan king, the bill of a duck.
A luck-drunken, lyrical, louche Fred Astaire
I am broke from your lavishiness, Mr Tim Clare.

If you've really a yen for identity theft,
finish the job then, take all that's left!
No, don't panic, I'm not going to call in 'the fuzz' –
you're a much better Tim Clare than I ever was.
Go on, take my smile!
Take the way that I sing!
Steal my dress sense, my walk,
come along, everything!
Get stuck in! Take my dandruff!
Here! Have my bad knee!
Come handcuff yourself
to my love of TV!
All my strange superstitions!
My lack of discretion!
My predisposition towards mild depression!
My disastrous dearth of finesse in the sack!
My fear that the ones I love most don't love back.
Fill your boots, until every last foible is gone.
You can be me, mate,
and I'll be no one.

Heart Of Class

Salt and vinegar of the earth
was how I used to take my women
that brackish tang
enough to set my trousers singing.
Teenage, lusty,
I set my sights on banging busty fitties
who won taxi-rank deathmatch fights
and spilt Stella on their titties.
Out for me! Out for me!
They all got 'em out for me!
Love was kebab alley bunk-ups
and woozy, queasy stuff
till one morning, I woke early
and I told the world... enough!

You see,
in every young man's life there comes a crossroads
where he may choose to face the demons in his mind,
and should the fripperies of youth turn to felicity and truth,
a change in temperament cannot be far behind.
And as I changed I recognised the grievous failings
amongst the sordid stripe of girl I'd tried to bed
but I broke free from the malaise,
resolved to mend my wicked ways,
and seek a higher calibre of mate instead.

O middle class girls!
Such a riddle class girls!
With regattas, ciabattas, sonatas each whirls!
So much richer than dustmen
yet poorer than earls!
Lovely middle class
middle class
middle class girls!

Do you thatch your own roof?
Is your money in stocks?
Do you find chips uncouth?
Do you call roosters 'cocks'?
Do you smoke on the sly?
Do you quaff too much plonk?
Is your favourite meal Thai?
Do you squeal when you bonk?
Is your veal all organic and aga-prepared?
Do you panic at lager and think French wine's *merde*?

Have you been to Uganda?
Is father well-read?
If I sponsor a panda
will you give me head?
Does bruschetta taste better with feta than brie?
Are you searching for merlot, and magic, and… me?

O middle class birds!
Make me dribble class birds!

Talk Fellini, Rossini, panini, hors d'oeuvres!
Stoke the fire in my loins
with a few foreign words!
Mighty middle class
middle class
middle class birds!

We'll talk art and sup Dubonnet
in a gallery, in Dunstable.
I'll 'show you the Monet'
If you'll show me your Constable.
I want to watch you kiss the glistening head
of programming at Radio 4,
ride a tide of broadsheet op-eds
until you're saddle-sore,
use a fish-knife like a lady
and a baster like whore.

Keep your fears apocalyptic
keep your *Times* Sudoku tricky
keep your *Guardian* crossword cryptic
Shun *The Mirror's* 'Tea Break Quicky.'
Splash our love across a triptych
quote quatrains until you're sticky
call me picky, but sweet Lord!

Mighty middle class chicks
(unlike Lidl class chicks)
look just thrilling refilling the low Bombay mix.

Let me glaze your visage
with the piddle that sticks!
Lovely middle class
middle class
middle class chicks.

Who needs love when there's Ikea?
Who needs joy when there's cocaine?
Who needs truth now Bluetooth's here?
We'll swap jpegs on the train!
Love's a poor investment dear
love will only cause you pain
relationships are so last year
must we go through this again?
Marriage forecasts all look gloomy
Cheer up! Here's some grilled halloumi!
My, this Volvo does feel roomy!
Drink some Zinfandel then screw me!

Say it's moral dereliction
spiritual constipation
don't you feel a strange conviction
that we're due some compensation?
See, we bear the same affliction
burdened with an education
all that's left's our shared addiction
hunger mixed with desperation.
Lust's a fire that leads to friction
friction sparks a conflagration

passion like the Crucifixion
rapture like the last salvation.
We both know that love's a fiction
romance – just an aberration
come, let's lie
with perfect diction
in endless mutual
masturbation.

Where's the Bundle?

The washerwoman had a bouncer's thick wrists
and the cracked, stained nails of a bookie;

every time she took out a fresh cigarette,
she placed the packet flat on the table

then slid it open like a trick drawer.
Her lighter clicked in the cave of her hands –

she guarded the secret of fire like a PIN.
A bird flew past the window, undulating crazily.

She spoke of moonlit liaisons with frogmen,
conversations mosaicked from multiple codewheels,

the Secret Santa of manila envelopes,
strictly no eye contact, except once,

reflected in a polished toecap.
She said the weathervane spun like a whirligig

(we pushed plectra under her fingernails)
like a punchdrunk bantamweight

like a dead sonar
(*more, more*) like God's swingball

like a blindfolded conjuror,
like an empty bottle (*there, that wasn't so hard*).

She said the courier turned, jockeyed his pushbike
up the dry rut of the drainage ditch,

spokey-dokeys rattling
like the knucklebones of saints.

To Mr T Seen From The Train

O why do you walk through the city in chains,
            missing so much and so much?
O sad black Adonis whom pity restrains,
why do you walk through the city in chains,
when the birds in the treetops sing pretty refrains
            and petrol tanks boom at your touch?
O why do you walk through the city in chains,
            missing so much and so much?

Dear Man I Saw On The Platform At Colchester

Dear man I saw on the platform at Colchester,
you hugged the ugly Polynesian girl
then waited while she got on board the train.
I confess, my knee-jerk thought was:
mail order bride.
With your drubbed face and imbecile fingers,
your lanky skittishness and
air of someone who smells like digestives
I thought:
who could love that
without a big fat cheque
and a chance to join the world's seventh largest
economy?

Dear man
I saw the tears in your eyes and thought:
fuckwit.
The girl took her seat a few rows from me
and in the crappy yellow light I wanted to stand and
yell:
Idiot man on the platform at Colchester
you are incapable of love.
You think your pain matters;
it does not.
Even the biggest boats

don't leave a dent when they exit the water.
This girl could lose her dismal face to a blender,
she could
stumble into a pit of lime or
dip her legs in a trash compactor
and no one would care
because your love is shabby and small.

Dear man,
when the train began to move, you,
like the worst cliché, started to follow,
and your walk became a canter became a clammy jog,
your unflattering blue Gortex coat and your three-tier
rucksack.
You ran
without a thought for dignity.
You ran
as if it mattered.

Dear man,
don't knock cowardice –
for years, it's been the only thing
keeping my wrists closed
and watching you run
I fancied you could do with a dose.
God knows
I'm a horrible cynic;
this grim armour
I hide behind, these shit-tinted specs,

all because deep down
Christ, I want to believe in things
but disappointment stings
and when I saw you drop your guard like that,
well,
I just wanted to protect you.

Dear man,
when you ran
you did not look like a twat.
Right then
you were beautiful
and I understood –
Joy is stupid
Hope runs for a train it can't catch
Passion sobs in the street and doesn't care who sees
Wisdom knows
sometimes it's okay
to drop the jaundiced swagger
and write a poem where you just say how you feel.

Dear man,
in a softer world
words would end here;
we'd wear their easy lesson like a superpower
stepping onto tracks
eyes closed
to stop locomotives with outstretched chin
and even if we failed

our last mistake would be so sweet.
We'd burst like great big Valentine hearts
to the singing of brakes
but you know
and I know
real life is not so glorious.
Please
don't confuse hope and hubris.

Dear man,
of course your love is small
that's how it fits
into each moment
and sure,
for all I know
you could be screwing her sister.
You could have gone home
and kicked the dog so hard in the kidneys
that it staggered like a sick beggar for two days before
dying –
it doesn't matter
because if hope exists
then like a book on a high shelf
it'll wait 'til we're ready
and if the universe isn't fair
maybe we'll all get more than we deserve.

Dear man, I saw
on the platform at Colchester:

a fool can taste such bliss
when every moment is a goodbye kiss.
All my days I've felt the lack of you,
that delinquent ache against the asphalt rain,
wax fruit hours that neither spoil nor satisfy,
a Dopplered heartbeat
like a disappearing train.

The Strange Death Of Charlie Wordsworth: Stand-Up Poet

i.

They laughed at him, rich, hearty laughs –
he wanted it at first,
he thrilled crowds at the open mic
with naughty, silly verse.

If you'd have asked his central themes
he would have answered: 'Crumbs.
I'd have to say the major seams
are death, the sea, and… bums.'

But poets are a contrary breed
who brood in draughty garrets,
the craft at which they most succeed
is making sticks from carrots.

Charles nursed a self-destructive streak
as sure as dogs can bark,
his insecurities, a gas leak,
waiting for a spark.

One night, at a recital
in a pub backroom in Dorking,
he walked into the venue late
and heard four poets talking.

'What's Wordsworth like?' the first one said.
His friends replied with curses:
'A nincompoop who's found a niche
For silly doggerel verses.'

'A tawdry novelty – it's just
as Dr Johnson said:
he's like a dog that's learned to walk
upon its hinder legs!'

'Yes, any fool can fluke a laugh
with rot about his bottom.
but who'll care in a hundred years?
No one! He'll be forgotten.'

Charles turned and left, his head hung low,
his heart felt small and sad
the poets' words rang in his ears,
they sounded like his Dad.

What was a grown man doing
writing sonnets to his anus?
What cares this world for silliness,
for stupid entertainers?

(Had he remembered Chaucer
then he might have had a better day –
a man for whom fart jokes in rhyme
were by and large a metier.)

Perhaps his 'Guffing Puffin' was
a *little* overzealous
perhaps the poets had a point
perhaps they were just jealous

but as it was, the seed was sown,
it took root in his heart,
he shut the door on botty-burps -
'From now – my work is *art*.'

ii.

Charles toiled with honest, vengeful vim,
he showed his craft what deference is.
Constructing jokes to shut out blokes
who didn't get the references.

At pubs and clubs and artsy hubs
his schtick could be relied on
to liven up the cabaret
with parodies of Dryden.

He even did impressions
'Ooh! He's just like that Rob Brydon!'
And yet, as his career thrived,
a dark tide rose inside him.

In every whoop, in each guffaw,
he heard a note of mockery,

oh sure, they found him *funny*
but they didn't listen properly.

'*This* is what those poets meant!
It's *these* fools who are stopping me!
I'm caged, and they're just visiting,
like Jail in Monopoly.'

His metre tightened like a noose,
his humour grew obscurer,
the artist on his shoulder
groomed the moustache of a Führer.
'An easy laugh's a *tainted* laugh –
We're after something... purer.'

As time went on (as is its wont)
his audience grew leaner
but when the door sales fell away
it only made him keener

and bit by bit his comedy
got cleverer and meaner.
His jokes had punchlines so abstruse
they might have been in Urdu:

'Oh, the time I've lost reading
A La Recherche Du Temps Perdu.'
A Proust pun? Ha! *Encore une fois*!
I don't know if they heard you!

He stripped the last gag from his act,
he read to dusty silence
'Not "stand-up poet" – "poet"!'
he'd insist with lusty violence.

He sent his work to journals,
he renamed his blog 'The Chronicle'
he wore his condescension
like a giant gilt-edged monocle.

He preened and puffed till, sure enough,
his swollen dream came true:
'We need a speaker, Charles – you game?
An invite-only do –

a small soiree to celebrate
our artform's finest minds.'
Charles tried to act all nonchalant:
'I'm… sure I'll find the time.'

The venue was a sombre place,
half-gallery, half-morgue.
The clientele looked dowdy – think
if Oxfam dressed the Borg.

The furrowedest of deeply-furrowed
brows had been invited
and underneath his cool façade
Charles was, in truth, excited.

A man stepped to the podium
in pallid, gulag chic,
he slurped a smidge of Pinot Grig
and then began to speak:

'It's wonderful to see so many of you here tonight
In this celebration of our country's finest,
most intelligent, most *vital* poets.
But before we get to our readers
we thought we'd start off with something a little lighter,
a little quirky. Ladies and gentlemen,
he's here to crack a few jokes, please welcome to the
stage
Charlie Wordsworth – the comedian.'

The words impaled Charles through the heart,
A hail of icy lances,
the editor and poets
trading matey, smirking glances.
He swore he heard one woman say:
'I wonder if he dances?'

His sheaf of weighty poems
now felt flimsy in his grasp
a dozen tatty betting slips
for horses that came last.

He teetered, for a moment,
then he lost himself to fate

from the ashes of rejection
rose a phoenix of pure hate

'I say...
        I say...
                I say...
                        I say...'
He said, to the assembled,
'I say... I say... I say... I say...'
And Zeus in Heaven trembled.

'I say... I say... I say... I say...'
His eyes flashed like a lion's.
'I say... I say... I say... I say...'
He spat, in perfect iambs.

'I say, I say, I say, I say,'
two words, both drenched in venom,
and in each pause, the rumble
of impending Armageddon.

'I say, I say, I say...
What do you get
If you cross a comedian
With a poet?

A MONGREL!' Came his anguished cry.
'A MONGREL!' Came the shout.

'Since thou art neither hot nor cold
Then God will spew thee out!

You want a joke? I'll tell you one!'
His pupils huge and wired,
'I've beat on brick walls all my life
And boy, are my arms tired!
A poet walks into a bar
and slowly falls apart
cos humans want anaesthetists
Not raw, trangressive art!

I say, I say, I say, I say,
What rots a man's heart faster?
The march of days and days and days
or mindless braying laughter?
That's not a gag. I'm asking you.
Please, someone – what's the answer?'

They dragged him from the podium
the mic fell slack and squealed
and back inside his hotel room
his tortured mind unpeeled.

iii.

Years passed; the pain gave way, at last,
to stanzas neat and measured,
no dropping pants, no farting grans,
no odes to goats he'd pleasured,
just lines like: 'brindled catfish / Haunt
these tides of Flemish weather.'

He lunched with noted critic
Bertrand Witsun-Goslingfeather,
talked shop while supping 12 year malts
that smelt of bottled leather,
when, finally, the moment
he'd been waiting for forever:
'I read your new collection, Charles.
It's really *very* clever.'

The words emerged, so small, so dry,
like spiders from a dustbin,
the words he'd spent years striving for –
He heard them...

                    and felt nothing.

See, joy is like a guinea pig,
it dies unless you feed it,
you might not notice that it's gone
until the day you need it

and sure, to court approval from
gourmets can be beguiling,
but work to please one frowning face
you lose the fifty smiling.

Don't kowtow to the tastemakers,
stand tall, although it rankles,
your heart worn proudly on your sleeve
your trousers round your ankles.

Acknowledgements

The author would like to thank Luke Wright, Ross Sutherland, Joe Dunthorne, Lisa Horton and his parents.

Also by Nasty Little Press

The Vile Ascent Of Lucien Gore And What The People Did
by Luke Wright
ISBN: 978-0-9563767-2-5 | £5

Boring The Arse Off Young People
by Martin Figura
ISBN: 978-0-9563767-3-2 | £5

Under The Pier
by Salena Godden
ISBN: 978-0-9563767-4-9 | £5

Whenever I Get Blown Up I Think Of You
by Molly Naylor
ISBN: 978-0-9563767-5-6 | £10

The New Blur Album
by John Osborne
ISBN: 978-0-9563767-7-0 | £5

Small Talk
by Nic Aubury
ISBN: 978-0-9563767-9-4 | £5

nastylittlepress.org